Beyond the Noise: Reclaim Your Inner Calm

Strategies and Techniques to Overcome Overthinking, Heighten Awareness, and Embrace the Present

Positive Thoughts

Contents

- Monitoring your thoughts

6. Meditation and Mindfulness

- The practice of mindfulness

- Meditation techniques for beginners

7. Mindful Breathing

- How breathing can influence your thoughts

- Breathing exercises

8. Practicing Gratitude

- Keeping a gratitude journal

- Focusing on the positive

9. Limiting Distractions

- Eliminating digital distractions

- Creating a quiet workspace

10. Setting Boundaries

- Saying "no" when necessary

- Learning to take time for yourself

11. Physical Exercise and Movement

- Benefits of sports and physical activity

- Specific mental exercises

12. Writing to Clear Your Mind

- Journaling and reflection

- Therapeutic writing techniques

13. Talking to Someone

- Finding a confidant

- Benefits of therapy

14. Time Management and Organization

- Planning techniques

- Avoiding procrastination

15. Learning to Embrace Uncertainty

- Letting go of the need for control

- Living in the present

16. Art and Creativity as an Outlet

1. Introduction

- Definition of "Overthinking"

"Overthinking" is the process of excessive, detailed, and prolonged analysis of decisions, situations, or problems. It's as if the mind can't detach from a particular thought, spiraling in a continuous cycle without reaching a conclusion or solution. Instead of allowing a natural flow of thoughts, the individual finds themselves trapped in a whirlwind of assumptions, "what if?" scenarios, and hypothetical situations.

This type of thinking can involve past events (ruminating on what could have been done differently), worries about the future (anxiety about what might happen), or even seemingly simple daily decisions (like choosing what to wear or eat).

The Effect of Excessive Rumination on Mental and Physical Health

Overthinking is not just a mental issue; it has tangible repercussions on an individual's overall health.

Mental Health:

- Overthinking can increase stress and anxiety levels. A mind constantly inundated with thoughts may exhibit symptoms such as insomnia, irritability, and difficulty concentrating.

- It can lead to issues like depression, anxiety, and obsessive-compulsive disorder (OCD). Continuous negative rumination can lower mood and lead to feelings of hopelessness and despair.

- Decision-making ability is compromised. A person who overthinks excessively may find themselves paralyzed by decisions, big or small, due to fear of making a mistake.

Physical Health:

- Chronic stress caused by overthinking can have negative effects on the body, such as raised blood pressure, digestive problems, or a weakened immune system.

- Sleep deprivation is a common side effect of overthinking. The inability to "switch off" the mind can lead to sleepless nights, which in turn can lead to health problems like obesity, heart disease, and diabetes.

- Muscle tension, headaches, and fatigue are other physical symptoms associated with overthinking.

Mental Health and Overthinking: Further Implications

Cognitive Fatigue: While the human mind is powerful and capable of processing an enormous amount of information, there's a limit to how much it can handle without consequences. Overthinking can lead to information overload and cognitive fatigue. This mental exhaustion can reduce the ability to think clearly, affecting learning and memory.

Self-esteem and Overthinking: Overthinking often involves self-doubt and negative self-reflection.

Over time, this can seriously damage an individual's self-esteem. When a person is constantly worried about not measuring up or making mistakes, they may begin to doubt their own abilities, leading to decreased self-confidence.

Relationships and Social Interactions: Continuous rumination can also affect personal relationships. A person who overthinks too much can become overly critical of themselves and others. They may start seeking signs of rejection or disapproval, even when they aren't present, compromising the quality of social interactions.

Physical Health and Overthinking: Prolonged Implications

Cardiovascular System: While anxiety and stress are known to raise blood pressure in the short term, chronic overthinking and prolonged stress can lead to long-term issues like hypertension. This condition, if uncontrolled, can increase the risk of heart disease and stroke.

Endocrine System: Prolonged stress can influence the endocrine system, leading to prolonged release of cortisol, the stress hormone. An excess of cortisol can affect metabolism, lead to weight gain, reduce immune function, and increase the risk of chronic diseases.

Digestive Health: Anxiety and stress can disrupt digestive function. Overthinking can lead to symptoms like nausea, diarrhea, constipation, and other digestive problems. In the long term, this can contribute to conditions like irritable bowel syndrome or gastric ulcers.

Musculoskeletal Health: As mentioned, overthinking can lead to muscle tension. However, in the long term, chronic tension can result in issues like chronic pain, backaches, and posture problems.

In conclusion, overthinking not only undermines our ability to function at our best mentally but also has tangible effects on our physical health. Understanding the breadth of its consequences can provide further motivation to seek strategies and techniques to address and overcome it.

2. Causes of Overthinking

- Past Events

Our brains have a natural ability to reflect on the past, helping us learn from our experiences and make better choices in the future. However, when this reflection becomes obsessive and repetitive, it can lead to overthinking.

Trauma and Negative Experiences: Traumatic events such as accidents, toxic relationships, or significant losses can leave a lasting impression in memory. These events can cause mental noise, with the individual continuously reliving the event while trying to find meaning, explanations, or imaginary solutions.

Regrets: Past decisions that led to negative outcomes can become constant sources of reflection. "What if" scenarios can dominate the mind, preventing the individual from accepting the present and moving forward.

Unresolved Interpersonal Conflicts:

- Disagreements with friends, family, or colleagues can be causes of overthinking, especially if they have not been resolved or openly discussed.

Fear of the Future:

- Anxiety about the future is another common cause of overthinking. The desire to control or predict unpredictable outcomes can lead to constant rumination.

- **Uncertainty:** We live in a constantly changing and uncertain world. Worries about financial stability, career, or health can trigger spirals of anxious thoughts.

- **High Expectations:** Both personal expectations and those imposed by society can create pressure. The fear of disappointing oneself or others can lead to constant reflection on future scenarios.

- **Avoidance:** Fear can also lead to avoiding certain situations. This avoidance can, in turn, fuel further thoughts about what might happen if the feared situation were to be confronted.

Perfectionism:

- Perfectionism is the relentless pursuit of excellence, often to the point of obsession. This mindset can often lead to overthinking.

- **Fear of Mistakes:** Perfectionists often fear making mistakes. They meticulously analyze every decision, worried about potential negative consequences, even if they are minimal.

- **Comparison:** Perfectionists tend to compare themselves to others, constantly measuring their own success against others. This can lead to continuous reflections on how to improve or what they might be doing "wrong."

- **Excessive Self-Criticism:** Even when a perfectionist achieves a goal, they may not feel satisfied, focusing on what they could have done better. This self-criticism can fuel overthinking and undermine self-esteem.

In summary, the causes of overthinking are complex and interconnected. Recognizing these causes is the first step in addressing them and finding effective strategies to manage and reduce overthinking.

Environment and Social Context:

- The environment in which we live and the social context can significantly impact our thought patterns.

- **Social Pressures:** Modern society is flooded with images of success, beauty, and apparent happiness, often conveyed through media and social networks. These representations can lead people to overthink their lives, comparing them to often unrealistic standards.

- **Culture of Multitasking:** We live in an era where we are often encouraged to do multiple things simultaneously. This sensory overload can lead the mind to constant rumination, trying to keep up with multiple demands.

- **Social Isolation:** Despite our increasingly digital connectivity, many people feel isolated. Loneliness can amplify internal thoughts, leading to cycles of overthinking.

Brain Biology and Chemistry:

- We cannot ignore the role of biology in the process of overthinking.

- **Brain Chemistry:** Neurochemical imbalances, particularly of neurotransmitters like serotonin and dopamine, can influence mood and thought patterns. These imbalances can predispose some individuals to anxiety and, consequently, overthinking.

- **Brain Structure:** Studies have shown that activity in certain areas of the brain, such as the anterior cingulate, can be correlated with obsessive-compulsive tendencies, including those of overthinking.

- **Genetics:** While overthinking as a trait is not directly inherited, a predisposition to mood or anxiety disorders, which can lead to excessive rumination, may have a genetic component.

Lifestyle and Daily Habits:

- Our daily routines can directly influence our propensity to overthink.

- **Lack of Sleep:** Sleep deprivation can negatively affect cognitive function, making it harder to regulate thoughts and exacerbating overthinking.

- **Stimulants:** Excessive use of caffeine and other stimulants can increase anxiety and, consequently, overthinking.

- **Lack of Physical Activity:** Physical exercise helps regulate neurotransmitters and reduce stress. A sedentary lifestyle can contribute to a higher incidence of overthinking.

Stress and Adaptability:

- Overthinking can also be a response to stress.

- **Stress Management:** Individuals who have not developed effective methods for managing stress may resort to overthinking as a defense mechanism, even if it is counterproductive.

- **Life Changes:** Significant events such as divorce, job loss, or illness can lead to intense and prolonged rumination.

Identifying and understanding the underlying causes of overthinking is crucial. Only by recognizing these roots can we hope to implement strategies to break these cycles and promote a healthier, more centered mindset.

Deep Psychological Aspects:

- Underlying psychological aspects can shed light on the motivations and mechanisms of overthinking.

- **Need for Control:** Psychologically, overthinking can stem from a deep need for control. Some individuals may feel that by intensely reflecting on a situation, they can predict or control the outcome, even if that is not realistically possible.

- **Defense Mechanisms:** Overthinking can be a defense mechanism against painful or traumatic emotions. Instead of facing these emotions, the individual may become fixated on details or hypothetical scenarios.

Relational and Communicative Dynamics:

- Dynamics within relationships can often be fertile ground for overthinking.

- **Ambiguous Communication:** If an individual receives ambiguous or mixed messages from someone important in their life, they may spend hours trying to "decode" hidden meanings or intentions.

- **Unexpressed Expectations:** Feeling the need to meet unspoken or perceived expectations can lead to reflections on how to fulfill them or the possible consequences of not doing so.

Cultural and Educational Background:

- The educational and cultural environments in which one grows up can have a lasting impact on thought patterns.

- **Rigid Education:** Growing up in an environment where mistakes are not tolerated can instill a fear of error and thus fuel overthinking.

- **Cultural Values:** Some cultures may emphasize reflection and introspection as virtues, while others may promote action and decision-making. Being in conflict with these cultural values can lead to endless rumination.

Work Environment:

- Overthinking can also be influenced by the type of work or workplace environment.

- **High Responsibilities:** Having a role that involves crucial decisions that can influence people's lives or have significant financial repercussions can lead to constant reflection.

- **Lack of Adequate Feedback:** Not receiving clear or regular feedback on one's work can leave room for individuals to question themselves and their decisions.

Comparison and Globalization

We live in a globalized world where we are constantly exposed to success stories from all around the globe.

Globalized Comparison: Every time we see someone succeeding in a similar area to ours, we might start reflecting on what we are doing, how we could do better, or what we could have done differently.

Continuous Access to Information: In a digital era, we are bombarded with information 24/7. This information overload can fuel overthinking as there's always a new piece of information to consider or analyze.

Recognizing the multiple causes of overthinking can help individuals identify specific problematic areas in their lives. This awareness is the first step in developing personalized strategies and targeted interventions to reduce overthinking and improve the quality of life.

3. The Connection Between Stress and Overthinking

How Stress Feeds Overthinking

Alert Response: Stress is a natural body reaction to situations perceived as threatening. When we feel under pressure or threatened, our brains go into an "alert" state, predisposing us to analysis. This response, once vital for our survival, can now translate into a tendency to overthink modern, less tangible challenges.

Feedback Loops: Stress can trigger overthinking, which in turn increases stress levels, creating a cycle of negative feedback. The more we think about a stressful problem or situation, the more anxious we become, fueling further rumination.

Avoidance: Faced with stress, some individuals may use overthinking as a means to avoid direct action. For example, if a person fears an upcoming job interview, they might spend hours pondering every possible scenario rather than preparing concretely or trying to relax.

The Body's Reaction to Overthinking

Fight or Flight Response: When overthinking a situation, the body may interpret this mental state as a threat, triggering the "fight or flight" response. This leads to a series of physiological changes, including increased heart rate, accelerated breathing, and muscle tension.

Cortisol: Overthinking can lead to increased cortisol production, the stress hormone. Elevated and prolonged cortisol levels can have negative health effects, including decreased immune function, digestive problems, and sleep disturbances.

Mental Exhaustion: Constant rumination can deplete mental resources. Like an overused muscle, the brain can become "tired," making it difficult to concentrate, make decisions, and process new information.

Sleep Issues: Overthinking, especially at night, can interfere with the ability to fall asleep and stay asleep. Sleep deprivation can then further exacerbate overthinking, creating another cycle of negative feedback.

Digestive Problems: What happens in the mind can have a direct impact on the body. Anxiety and stress associated with overthinking can lead to digestive issues such as acidity, indigestion, or gastrointestinal disturbances.

Associated Disorders

Many psychological conditions can have both stress and overthinking as concurrent symptoms or triggering factors.

Anxiety Disorders: Overthinking is often associated with generalized anxiety disorders, panic attacks, and specific phobias. In these conditions, individuals can become preoccupied and obsessed with particular thoughts or scenarios, fueling further levels of anxiety.

Depression: While depression may manifest with symptoms of lethargy or apathy, many people with depression also experience intense periods of overthinking. These thoughts may concern self-esteem, guilt, or regrets.

Environmental Factors

External stimuli can influence our stress levels and, consequently, our inclination to overthink.

Overstimulation: We live in an era of constant information. Being continuously exposed to news, social media, and interruptions can keep the brain in a hyperactive state, favoring overthinking.

Noise and Pollution: Studies have shown that exposure to high levels of noise or pollution can increase stress levels, creating fertile ground for overthinking.

Rumination vs. Reflection

While overthinking is often seen as negative, it is essential to distinguish between rumination and reflection.

Rumination: Rumination is a type of overthinking in which the individual gets stuck in a cycle of negative thoughts, often concerning past events or future worries. This type of thinking can be harmful and paralyzing.

Reflection: On the other hand, reflection is a type of deep and considered thought that can lead to new insights and resolutions. Reflection can be a way to process emotions and experiences constructively.

Long-Term Health Impact

Prolonged overthinking and the resulting stress do not only have short-term effects; they can also have long-term health repercussions.

Immune System: As mentioned, elevated cortisol production can weaken the immune system, making individuals more susceptible to illnesses and infections.

Cardiovascular Health: Chronic stress and tension associated with overthinking can increase the risk of cardiovascular problems, such as hypertension and heart diseases.

Cognitive Health: Continued exposure to stress and overthinking can negatively impact cognitive function, potentially increasing the risk of conditions like dementia in later life.

The Emotional Connection

The link between emotions and overthinking is profound. Intense feelings, such as sadness or anger, can trigger periods of excessive rumination.

Emotional Processing: Some individuals use overthinking as a means to process emotions. However, if not managed properly, this process can become counterproductive, causing further increases in stress and negative emotions.

Understanding the connection between stress and overthinking and the numerous factors that can influence this relationship is essential for developing effective management strategies and protecting mental and physical health. Awareness of these connections and their implications can guide individuals toward more targeted interventions and a higher quality of life.

Inhibition of Creativity and Problem-Solving

Creative Block: Overthinking can put the brakes on the creative process. While a certain amount of stress can actually enhance performance, an excess of stress and rumination can make individuals feel stuck, unable to generate new ideas or solutions.

Reduced Mindfulness: Overthinking can also divert attention away from the "here and now," making it challenging to address problems effectively. If the mind is engaged in constant cycles of reflection and worry, the ability to solve problems creatively is compromised.

Relational Health and Social Connections

Emotional Withdrawal: Overthinking and related stress can lead to emotional withdrawal, as individuals become so wrapped up in their thoughts that they disconnect from people around them.

Misunderstandings: In a state of overthinking, it's easy to misinterpret the words and actions of others, contributing to further stress. This can lead to unnecessary conflicts and tensions in relationships.

Temporal Aspects and Life Cycles

Impact on Time Perception: Stress and overthinking can distort our perception of time. When immersed in anxious thoughts, time may seem to pass more slowly, creating additional levels of stress.

Critical Life Moments: Periods of significant change or important decisions can exacerbate both stress and overthinking. For example, during life transitions like graduation, marriage, or the birth of a child, people are more inclined to overthink what could go wrong, fueling stress.

Impact on Performance and Self-Esteem

Analysis Paralysis: In the workplace or academia, overthinking can lead to what is commonly known as "analysis paralysis," where a person becomes so engrossed in pondering every detail that they become incapable of making any decision.

Self-Esteem: Overthinking can lead to a negative spiral of self-doubt. Individuals may begin to question their own abilities, which can further erode self-esteem and, consequently, increase stress.

Other Mental Health Disorders

Overlap with Other Disorders: Overthinking is not just an isolated phenomenon; it is often linked to other mental health disorders such as depression, anxiety disorders, and obsessive-compulsive disorders. Stress can act as a catalyst, exacerbating the symptoms of these disorders.

The connection between stress and overthinking is intricate, with multiple layers of interaction that can significantly impact an individual's quality of life. A profound understanding of this relationship is crucial for developing therapeutic strategies and effective interventions that can help people break free from the trap of overthinking and lead a more serene and fulfilling life.

4. The Negative Cycle of Overthinking

How it Starts and Self-Perpetuates

External Triggers: Overthinking often originates from external stimuli or situations. These can include a casual comment made by a colleague, distressing news, or an unexpected event. Instead of processing and letting go of this information, the mind begins to fixate on it.

Internal Noise: Lingering thoughts and worries can emerge without a clear external stimulus. An old regret or a fear of the future can trigger a cycle of overthinking.

Individual Predisposition: Some people are naturally more inclined toward reflection and analysis. This tendency, if left unchecked, can easily turn into overthinking.

Amplification: Once a thought or worry has taken hold, the mind can amplify it. What started as a minor concern becomes a catastrophic scenario, fueling further anxiety and worry.

The Downward Spiral

Narrowed Focus: As overthinking intensifies, the individual may start to exclusively focus on negative thoughts, excluding any other thoughts or perspectives.

Background Noise: Over time, these dominant thoughts can become constant "background noise," making it difficult to concentrate on anything else or make rational decisions.

Avoidance: To try to manage the distress arising from overthinking, an individual might begin to avoid situations, people, or activities they believe could trigger further negative thoughts. This avoidance can limit life experiences and further isolate the person.

Physical Effects: As mentioned earlier, overthinking doesn't just affect the mind but also the body. These physical effects (such as insomnia, muscle tension, etc.) can, in turn, reinforce the cycle of overthinking.

Reinforcing Limiting Beliefs: Overthinking often reinforces limiting beliefs about oneself and the surrounding world. For example, if someone constantly thinks, "I'm not good enough," these reflections can further root this belief, making it even more challenging to challenge or overcome.

Exacerbation of Issues: Paradoxically, while overthinking may originate from a desire to solve or avoid problems, it can actually worsen them. For example, excessive worrying about a relationship can create tensions or misunderstandings that didn't exist before.

Cognitive Distortions:

Overgeneralization: A single negative experience is seen as a pattern of failure. For example, making a mistake in a project can lead to the belief: "I always mess everything up."

Mental Filter: This is the tendency to exclusively focus on the negative aspects of a situation, completely ignoring the positives. If ten things go well and one goes wrong, the overthinker will focus solely on the negative.

Catastrophizing: Here, the individual always imagines the worst possible scenario. A minor worry, like a headache, can turn into a fear of a severe illness.

Emotional Repercussions:

Feelings of Helplessness: One of the most devastating consequences of overthinking is the sense of helplessness. When constantly thinking about problems without taking action, one can begin to feel that the situation is out of control.

Emotional Isolation: Too many thoughts can create a barrier between the individual and others. The overthinker may feel that no one can understand or relate to their incessant thoughts.

Effects on Decision-Making Ability:

Procrastination: Overthinking can lead to decision paralysis, where the fear of making the wrong choice results in no decision being made.

Lack of Confidence: Constant second-guessing of oneself can erode confidence in one's judgment, making it difficult to trust one's decisions.

Environmental and Cultural Influences:

Information Culture: We live in an age where we are bombarded with information. This overload can fuel overthinking as we try to process and analyze every piece of information.

Social Comparison: Social media can exacerbate overthinking. Seeing highlights of someone else's life can lead us to overthink our own lives, choices, and paths.

The Persistence of the Cycle:

Negative Feedback Loop: Like a snake eating its tail, each round of overthinking reinforces the cycle.

Anxious thoughts generate more stress, leading to further anxious thoughts.

External Reinforcements: Sometimes, the environment or people around you can unintentionally reinforce overthinking. For example, an excessively worried parent can pass on this behavior to their children.

Overthinking, as can be seen, is not just a habit or personality trait but a complex interweaving of cognitive, emotional, and behavioral reactions. Breaking the cycle of overthinking requires a multifaceted approach that addresses the roots and manifestations of this behavior.

5. Recognizing When You're "Overthinking"

Signs and Symptoms:

- **Repetitive Thoughts:** You find yourself constantly revisiting the same situations, conversations, or decisions without reaching a conclusion or solution.

- **Insomnia:** Difficulty falling asleep or waking up in the middle of the night with a racing mind are often signs of overthinking.

- **Anxiety or Feelings of Overwhelm:** A growing sense of worry, restlessness, or nervousness, especially when there is no immediate or obvious reason for these feelings.

- **Decision Difficulty:** Feeling that every decision, even everyday and trivial ones, requires excessive analysis.

- **Ruminating on the Past:** Dwelling on past mistakes, embarrassments, or awkward moments, repeatedly replaying them.

- **Excessive Future Concern:** Constantly worrying about what might happen, imagining negative or catastrophic scenarios.

- **Lack of Action:** Finding yourself paralyzed or reluctant to move forward on a task or decision due to overwhelming thoughts.

- **Distraction:** Having difficulty concentrating on a single activity because your mind is elsewhere.

Monitoring Your Thoughts:

- **Thought Journal:** Keeping a journal can help you identify overthinking patterns. Write down your thoughts and feelings, and note the circumstances that seem to trigger overthinking.

- **Feedback from Others:** People around you may notice if you're getting lost in your thoughts. Ask them to let you know if they see you becoming overly analytical or worried.

- **Mindfulness and Meditation:** Practicing mindfulness helps you become more aware of your thoughts and feelings in the present moment. This awareness can help you recognize when you're slipping into overthinking.

- **Reflection Pause:** If you notice you're stuck in a cycle of thoughts, take a moment to pause and assess. Ask yourself, "Am I overthinking right now? Are these thoughts productive?"

- **Limit Exposure to Triggers:** If you notice that certain stimuli, like news or social media, fuel your overthinking, limit your exposure to them. Set specific times to check these channels or take digital breaks.

Recognizing overthinking is the crucial first step in addressing it. With increased awareness, you can begin to take steps to break the cycle and reduce the negative impact it has on your life.

Physical Manifestations of Overthinking:

- **Muscle Tension:** When caught in the overthinking whirlwind, you may notice muscles, especially those in the neck, shoulders, or back, becoming tense. This tension can lead to headaches or other muscle pains.

- **Changes in Breathing:** Shallow or accelerated breathing can be a sign that your mind is racing.

- **Upset Stomach:** Anxiety and worry stemming from overthinking can manifest as digestive disturbances, like stomachaches or acid reflux.

Behavioral Changes:

- **Avoidance:** You may start avoiding situations or people you fear could trigger further overthinking, thus limiting your interactions and experiences.

- **Procrastination:** Overthinking can lead to delaying decisions or actions in an attempt to have "more time to think," which can further exacerbate the cycle of overthinking.

- **Compulsiveness:** Some may react to overthinking by seeking control through compulsive behaviors, such as repeatedly checking things or organizing obsessively.

Time Assessment:

- **Temporal Focus of Thoughts:** If you constantly find yourself fixated on the past or worried about the future rather than living in the present, it might be a sign of overthinking.

- **Time Dilation:** Hours can feel like minutes when you're immersed in an overthinking cycle, with time seeming to slip away unnoticed.

Self-Assessment Tools:

- **Mood Tracking Apps:** There are many available apps that allow you to record your mood and associated thoughts, helping you identify when and why you might be slipping into overthinking.

- **Grounding Techniques:** These techniques, like the "5-4-3-2-1 technique," can help you reconnect with the present moment when you feel overwhelmed by thoughts. They are particularly useful for interrupting the cycle of overthinking when you recognize it.

- **Questionnaires and Tests:** Various psychological questionnaires and self-diagnostic tests can help you recognize and assess the extent of your overthinking.

Comparison with Others:

- **Support Groups:** Participating in anxiety or overthinking support groups can offer an external perspective. Listening to others' experiences can help you recognize signs of overthinking in your life.

Recognizing overthinking may take time and practice, especially if it has become a habit or an automatic reaction. However, with awareness and the right tools, you can identify it and begin to take steps to reduce or manage it effectively.

Quantitative Measures:

- **Time Tracking:** Use a timer or time-tracking app to record how much time you actually spend thinking about a particular problem or situation. Seeing time "in numbers" can be an alarm signal.

- **Intensity Scale:** Create a scale from 1 to 10 to assess the intensity of your thoughts. If you frequently find yourself exceeding level 7, it's a clear sign that you're overthinking.

Psychosomatic Signs:

- **Muscle Tension:** If you notice muscle tension, especially in the neck, shoulders, or jaw, it could be a physical sign of overthinking.

- **Increased Heart Rate:** Anxiety generated by overthinking can manifest through an elevated heart rate or palpitations.

- **Digestive Disturbances:** Stress and anxiety can affect the digestive system, leading to symptoms like nausea or gastrointestinal issues.

Effects on Relationships:

- **Superficial Conversations:** If you find yourself avoiding deep or meaningful conversations for fear of saying the wrong thing or being judged, it could be a sign of overthinking.

- **Social Withdrawal:** The desire to avoid potential stress triggers can lead you to distance yourself from friends and family.

Indirect Signs:

- **Procrastination:** Overthinking can lead to procrastination as a defense mechanism to avoid decisions or actions that could trigger further stress.

- **Perfectionism:** Feeling that every detail must be analyzed and optimized can be a symptom of overthinking.

- **Self-Criticism:** If you find that your internal dialogue is predominantly critical and relentless, you're likely falling into the overthinking trap.

Self-Inquiry Techniques:

- **Direct Questions:** Asking questions like "What's the worst-case scenario that could happen?" or "Will this matter in five years?" can help evaluate the severity and relevance of your thoughts.

- **SWOT Analysis:** Try conducting a Strengths, Weaknesses, Opportunities, and Threats (SWOT) analysis regarding the issue you're overthinking. This can offer a more balanced view of the situation.

6. Meditation and Mindfulness

Practice of Mindfulness:

Definition of Mindfulness: Mindfulness, or awareness, refers to the practice of being fully present and engaged in the moment, without judgment. It involves observing your thoughts and feelings without trying to change them or react to them.

Benefits of Mindfulness:

- **Stress Reduction:** It helps calm the mind, reducing anxiety and panic.

- **Increased Concentration:** Enhances the ability to focus on specific tasks, reducing distractions.

- **Greater Emotional Connection:** Promotes a deeper understanding of your emotions and how to respond to them.

Daily Mindfulness Practices:

- **Mindful Observation:** Pay attention to daily activities like eating, walking, or breathing. For instance, when you eat, notice flavors, textures, and aromas.

- **Active Listening:** When conversing with someone, fully focus on what they're saying without thinking about your response.

Meditation Techniques for Beginners:

- **Breath Awareness Meditation:**

  1. Sit in a comfortable position with a straight back.

  2. Close your eyes and bring your attention to your breath.

  3. Observe the sensation of air entering and leaving your nostrils.

  4. When the mind wanders, gently acknowledge the distraction and return your focus to your breath.

- **Guided Meditation:**

- Listen to recordings or use apps that guide you through a meditation session.

    - These often include visualizations, progressive relaxation, and other techniques to help center the mind.

- **Walking Meditation:**

    - Walk slowly and mindfully, noticing each footstep as it touches the ground.

    - Feel the connection between your foot and the earth, staying aware of each step.

- **Loving-Kindness Meditation (Metta):**

    1. Begin by focusing attention on your breath.

    2. Slowly start sending thoughts of love and kindness to yourself: "May I be happy. May I be at peace."

    3. Extend these thoughts of love and kindness to others, including friends, family, and even strangers or enemies.

- **Body Scan Meditation:**

    1. Sit or lie down in a comfortable position.

    2. Start from your feet and slowly move up through each part of your body, noticing any sensations, warmth, cold, or tension.

    3. The goal is to observe without judgment or an attempt to change what you feel.

Meditation and mindfulness are powerful tools for breaking the cycle of overthinking. Through these practices, you learn not to attach to thoughts and see them for what they are: passing mental events. Over time and with regular practice, you can develop a calmer and more centered mind, significantly reducing the impulse to overthink.

Tools and Settings for Meditation:

- **Cushions and Benches:** Using special cushions or benches for meditation can help maintain a correct posture and feel more comfortable during longer sessions.

- **Environment:** Creating a dedicated meditation space in your home can reinforce your practice. It doesn't need to be an entire room; a quiet corner with a candle or some stones can suffice.

- **Music and Sounds:** Many find it helpful to meditate with background sounds like waves, chants, rain, or forest sounds. There are numerous apps and recordings that offer these sounds.

Mindfulness in Daily Activities:

- **Mindful Eating:** Take the time to savor every bite of food. Notice the texture, taste, and how it makes you feel. This practice not only reduces overthinking but can also help with digestion and satiety.

- **Mindful Shower:** Focus on the sensation of water on your skin, the scent of soap, and the sound of water. Turn a daily routine into a meditative moment.

- **Mindful Listening:** When in conversation, instead of thinking about what you'll say next, truly concentrate on what the other person is saying.

Depth of Meditation:

- **Transcending the Self:** With deep practice, you can begin to feel a connection to something greater than yourself. This sense of unity can help put small problems or worries into perspective.

- **Realization of Impermanence:** Meditation can lead you to recognize that everything, including your thoughts, is temporary. This realization can help you let go of persistent or obsessive thoughts.

Obstacles and Challenges in Meditation:

- **Frustration:** It's common to feel frustrated when the mind keeps wandering during meditation. It's important to remember that the practice isn't about "emptying the mind" but rather noticing when the mind drifts and gently bringing it back to the present.

- **Impatience:** Many expect immediate results from meditation. However, like any other skill, it requires practice and persistence.

- **Posture:** Maintaining proper posture can be challenging, especially for beginners. It's helpful to start with short sessions and, if necessary, use cushions or benches to support your back.

Additional Resources:

Consider the idea of attending meditation retreats or workshops to deepen your practice. Additionally, there are many books and online courses that can provide detailed instructions and insights into meditation and mindfulness.

In summary, integrating meditation and mindfulness into daily life can offer a powerful antidote to overthinking, bringing greater peace, clarity, and joy to your everyday experiences.

7. Mindful Breathing:

How Breath Can Influence Your Thoughts:

- **Mind-Body Connection:** Breath is the only autonomous system of the body that can be easily controlled. Therefore, it can serve as a bridge between the mind and the body, influencing both simultaneously.

- **Stress Response Reduction:** Deep and rhythmic breathing can activate the parasympathetic nervous system, responsible for the body's "rest and digest" response. This can help calm an anxious mind and reduce the effects of stress.

- **Focus and Concentration:** Regular and controlled breathing can help clear the mind, facilitating concentration and reducing distractibility.

- **Emotional Regulation:** When we are emotionally agitated, our breath tends to be irregular or shallow. Bringing awareness to the breath can help stabilize our emotions.

Breathing Exercises:

1. **Abdominal Breathing:**

   - Sit or lie down in a comfortable position.

   - Place one hand on your chest and the other on your stomach.

   - Inhale slowly through the nose, allowing the stomach to expand (the hand on the chest should remain still).

   - Exhale slowly through the mouth or nose, feeling the stomach contract.

   - Repeat for at least 5-10 minutes.

2. **4-7-8 Breathing:**

- Sit with a straight back.

- Close your mouth and silently inhale through the nose counting to 4.

- Hold your breath for a count of 7.

- Exhale completely through the mouth with a whooshing sound for a count of 8.

- This is one breath. Now, repeat the cycle three more times for a total of four breaths.

3. **Alternate Nostril Breathing (Nadi Shodhana):**

- Sit comfortably with a straight back.

- Use your right thumb to close your right nostril.

- Inhale deeply through the left nostril.

- Now, close the left nostril with your ring and pinky fingers, and open the right nostril.

- Exhale through the right nostril, then inhale through the same nostril.

- Close the right nostril and open the left, then exhale through the left nostril.

- This completes one cycle. Continue for at least 5-10 cycles.

4. **Square Breathing:**

- Sit comfortably.

- Inhale for a count of 4.

- Hold your breath for a count of 4.

- Exhale for a count of 4.

- Keep your lungs empty for a count of 4.

- Repeat for at least 5 minutes.

By incorporating these breathing exercises into your daily routine, you can develop greater awareness and control over your mental state. With practice, you will find it easier to return to a center of calm and clarity, even in moments of stress or turmoil.

The Ancient Wisdom of Breath:

The practice of focusing on the breath has ancient roots and is found in many spiritual and cultural traditions. Buddhist monks, for example, use breath as a primary tool in their meditation practice. Also in the field of yoga, "pranayama" or breath control is fundamental.

Breath and Physiology:

- **Heart Rate and Breath:** When we breathe deeply and rhythmically, our heartbeat can synchronize, a phenomenon known as heart coherence. This synchronization has beneficial effects on the body, such as reducing blood pressure.

- **Brain Oxygenation:** Deep and mindful breathing ensures better oxygenation of the brain, promoting mental clarity and improved cognitive function.

The Art of Breath in Daily Life:

- **Breath During Activities:** Whether you are exercising, cooking, or simply walking, becoming aware of your breath can transform an ordinary activity into a meditative opportunity.

- **Breath and Eating:** Practicing mindful breathing before meals can aid digestion. Taking a moment to breathe deeply and express gratitude for the food in front of you can bring greater awareness and gratitude to your eating experience.

Additional Breath Exercises:

5. **Fire Breath (Kapalbhati):**

   - Sit in a comfortable position with a straight back.

   - Begin with a deep breath.

   - Exhale forcefully and rapidly through the nose, contracting the abdominal muscles.

- Let inhalation occur naturally and effortlessly.

- Continue for 15-30 seconds and then slow down to return to normal breathing.

6. **Breath Contemplation:**

   - Find a quiet place to sit or lie down.

   - Instead of altering your breath, simply observe it. Notice the temperature, rhythm, and any other details.

   - When the mind wanders, gently return to observing the breath.

7. **Counted Breathing:**

   - Sit in a comfortable position.

   - Inhale for a count of 5.

   - Hold for a count of 3.

   - Exhale slowly for a count of 7.

   - Repeat for at least 5-10 minutes.

Breath and Social Interaction:

Paying attention to your breath during social interactions can help you stay centered and present. If you find yourself in a stressful or difficult conversation, taking a few deep breaths can help you respond with greater calm and reflection.

In conclusion, breath is much more than an automatic bodily function: it is a powerful key to our mental and physical health. By cultivating a practice of mindful breathing, we can access a deep sense of peace and well-being wherever we are.

8. The Practice of Gratitude:

The Power of Gratitude:

Gratitude is not just a simple expression of thanks; it is a powerful catalyst for well-being. It can improve mood, reduce stress, and help develop a more positive outlook on life.

Science and Gratitude:

Studies have shown that people who regularly practice gratitude have reduced stress levels, better sleep quality, and greater life satisfaction. They have also demonstrated a stronger immune system and a lower likelihood of developing depressive disorders.

Keeping a Gratitude Journal:

Benefits: Having a dedicated place to record what you are grateful for can serve as a tangible reminder of the beauty and joys of life, even in difficult times.

Getting Started:

- Choose a journal or notebook you like.

- Set aside a specific time each day, perhaps before bedtime, to reflect and write.

- Record three things you are grateful for that day. No matter how big or small.

- Try to avoid repetitions; this will encourage deeper reflection and noticing the small positive details of your life.

Focusing on the Positive:

Mind Recalibration: Often, the human mind is tuned to notice what is wrong or lacking in our lives, an evolutionary legacy called "negativity bias." The practice of gratitude can help us recalibrate our attention, placing greater emphasis on the positive.

Gratitude Jar Exercise:

- Take an empty jar and small paper notes.

- Each day, write down something positive that happened or something you're grateful for on a note.

- Place the note in the jar.

- At the end of the year or when you're feeling down, open the jar and read the notes to remind yourself of positive moments.

Gratitude in Daily Life:

Take a pause during the day to stop and appreciate what surrounds you. It can be something as simple as the sun shining, birds singing, or a smile from a stranger. These small moments of appreciation can add up and have a significant impact on your overall perception of life.

By incorporating the practice of gratitude into your daily life, you will find it easier to focus on life's joys and beauties rather than its obstacles. This attitude can not only improve your mental health but also positively influence those around you, creating a virtuous cycle of positivity.

The Neuroscience of Gratitude:

Gratitude has measurable effects on the brain. Neuroimaging studies have shown that expressing gratitude activates the hypothalamus, a part of the brain that regulates various essential bodily functions, including appetite, sleep, and stress production. This suggests that gratitude may have beneficial effects on overall well-being and how we respond to stress.

Furthermore, gratitude is associated with the activation of brain regions related to reward systems, releasing neurotransmitters like dopamine, which produce feelings of pleasure and contentment.

The "Boomerang" Effect of Gratitude:

When we show gratitude, we often set off a chain reaction. Expressing appreciation can encourage others to do the same, creating an atmosphere of reciprocity and connection. This strengthening of social relationships can further contribute to our well-being.

Gratitude in Challenging Times:

While it's easy to feel grateful when everything is going well, it's in difficult moments that gratitude can be particularly powerful. Recognizing small blessings or lessons learned during tough times can help transform your perception of challenges and find strength and hope.

"Reframed Perception" Exercise:

Reflect on a recent or past challenge in your life. Instead of focusing on the negative aspects, ask yourself, "What have I learned from this experience? Is there something to be grateful for, despite the difficulty?" Write down your reflections, focusing on the positive aspects or lessons learned.

Gratitude as a Way of Life:

Integrating gratitude into your daily routine can turn it into a way of life. Rather than viewing gratitude as an isolated activity, it can become a way of living and perceiving the world.

The "Gratitude Walk" Exercise:

During your daily walk, set the intention to notice and appreciate the little things around you. It could be the beauty of nature, a kind gesture from a stranger, or simply the feeling of the sun on your skin. With each step, strengthen your connection to the present and nurture a sense of gratitude for the experience.

Conclusion:

Gratitude, when practiced with awareness and intention, has the power to transform not only our internal perception but also our external interactions. Through exercises, reflections, and dedicated daily practice, we can cultivate a deep sense of appreciation that permeates every aspect of our lives, leading to greater joy, connection, and overall well-being.

9. Limiting Distractions:

The Cost of Distractions:

We live in an era where distractions are commonplace. A notification on your smartphone, an incoming email, a new episode of your favorite TV series – all these things vie for our attention. And while these distractions may seem harmless, they actually come at a cost. Besides compromising our productivity, they can also fuel overthinking, diverting us from the present moment and fragmenting our attention.

Eliminating Digital Distractions:

1. Minimize Notifications:

Disable all non-essential notifications on your phone or computer. This includes social media apps, games, and news. If a notification doesn't pertain to a call or a message directly addressed to you, consider if you truly need it.

2. **Digital Detox:**

Dedicate a few hours each day or even a whole day each week away from electronic devices. Use this time to read, meditate, take walks, or engage in other offline activities.

3. **Monitoring Apps:**

Utilize apps like "Forest" or "Focus@Will" to track and limit time spent on specific apps or websites. These applications help you stay focused, reducing the temptation to impulsively browse.

Creating a Quiet Workspace:

1. **Personalize Your Space:**

Dedicate a specific area of your home or office as a workspace. When you're there, your brain recognizes it's time to focus.

2. **Remove Visual Distractions:**

Keep your desk and workspace tidy and free of unnecessary items. A clean and organized environment can reduce the feeling of chaos and enhance concentration.

3. **Use Headphones:**

If you're in a noisy environment, wear headphones to cancel out noise or listen to relaxing music that might help you concentrate.

4. **Scheduled Breaks:**

Work in time blocks, such as 25 minutes of work followed by a 5-minute break. This method, also known as the Pomodoro technique, can help maintain high focus and provide regular moments to relax and recharge.

5. **Physical Environment:**

Consider lighting, temperature, and the comfort of your chair and desk. A comfortable environment can make a significant difference in your ability to concentrate.

The Psychology of Distractions:

Distractions are not just external impediments; often, our internal predisposition plays a crucial role in making these distractions effective. Understanding the psychology of distractions can provide tools to combat them more effectively.

1. **Curiosity vs. Necessity:**

Often, we allow ourselves to be distracted not because we need that information but because our minds are naturally curious. Recognizing this difference can help resist the urge to check every notification or update.

2. **Emotional Avoidance:**

Sometimes, we distract ourselves to avoid dealing with challenging emotions or tasks. Recognizing when you're using distractions as a defense mechanism can enable you to confront what you're avoiding directly.

In-Depth Look at Digital Distractions:

1. **Endless Scrolling:**

Many websites and apps, particularly social media, employ "endless scrolling" to keep users engaged as long as possible. Being aware of this tactic can help you break the habit.

2. **Nighttime Digital Detox:**

Avoid using electronic devices at least an hour before bedtime. This can improve sleep quality and reduce nighttime anxiety and overthinking.

Advanced Strategies for Creating a Quiet Workspace:

1. **Colors and Mood:**

The colors in your workspace can influence your mood and productivity. Shades like blue and green are often considered relaxing and can promote concentration.

2. **Indoor Plants:**

Plants not only improve air quality but can also reduce stress and increase productivity. Consider adding some indoor plants like snake plants or pothos to your workspace.

3. **No-Tech Zones:**

Designate certain areas of your home as tech-free zones. These can be places for reading, meditating, or simply relaxing without digital devices.

4. **Workday Rituals:**

Establish a ritual to start your workday, such as a few minutes of deep breathing or journaling. This can help you get into a focused mindset and reduce distractions throughout the day.

Techniques to Support Deep Concentration:

1. **Concentration Training:**

Just like any other muscle, your ability to concentrate can be strengthened with regular practice. Dedicate periods of time each day for uninterrupted reading, studying, or working.

2. **Concentration Meditation:**

There are specific meditations, like Shamatha meditation, that are directly aimed at improving concentration. These practices can help you develop greater resistance to distractions.

Conclusion:

In an increasingly interconnected world, the ability to limit distractions has become a valuable skill. Through a combination of psychological understanding, environmental strategies, and regular practice, we can cultivate a space and a mental state that promotes deep concentration and overall well-being.

10. Setting Boundaries

The Importance of Boundaries in Our Modern World:

We live in an age of hyperconnectivity where we're expected to be always available and responsive. While this can bring benefits in terms of communication and access to information, it also has the potential to overwhelm our minds, increasing the risk of overthinking. Setting clear boundaries has become essential not only to protect our time and energy but also to preserve our mental health.

Saying "No" When Necessary:

1. **The Power of "No":**

Saying "no" is not just a rejection of something; it's also an affirmation of autonomy and priorities. It allows you to safeguard your time, energy, and well-being.

2. **Guilt-Free "No":**

Many of us struggle with guilt when saying "no." It's essential to recognize that setting boundaries is a right, not a privilege. There's no obligation to justify yourself every time.

3. **Techniques for Saying "No":**

Practice gentle yet firm ways to decline requests or offers. For example: "Thank you for offering, but I can't accept at this time."

Learning to Take Time for Yourself:

1. **Self-Renewal:**

Time for yourself isn't a luxury; it's a necessity. It serves to recharge, reflect, and reconnect with your needs and desires.

2. **Create Personalized Rituals:**

Whether it's reading a book, taking a walk, meditating, or listening to music, find what helps you relax and dedicate time to it every day.

3. **Scheduling "Me" Time:**

Just as you schedule meetings and activities, you should also schedule moments solely for yourself. This can be an effective way to ensure you have the time needed to recharge.

4. **Designate Personal Spaces:**

If possible, create a corner or a room in your home dedicated exclusively to relaxation and rejuvenation. This can become a refuge from external chaos and a place to reconnect with yourself.

5. **Connect with Nature:**

Spending time outdoors, whether it's a short walk in the park or a mountain getaway, can have profoundly rejuvenating effects on the mind and body. Nature can help break the cycle of overthinking and restore a sense of balance.

The Social Context of Boundaries:

In many cultures, especially in competitive work environments, there's subtle social pressure to always say "yes." This can stem from the fear of missing out on opportunities or the desire to appear as a team player. However, when prioritizing others' needs over your own, you risk losing sight of what truly matters.

The Art of Saying "No" and Its Facets:

1. **Saying "No" with Empathy:**

The key to gently refusing is appealing to empathy. Help people understand that your decision isn't a personal rejection but a necessity for your well-being.

2. **"No" as an Act of Self-Love:**

Every time you set a boundary, you're practicing self-love. You're acknowledging that your time, energy, and well-being are precious.

3. **The Importance of Timing:**

If you know you'll need to decline something, try to do so in advance. This gives others time to adjust or find alternatives.

Taking Time for Yourself and the Psychological Benefits:

1. **Mental Regeneration:**

Like a machine that needs to be turned off and restarted, our brains require regular breaks. This allows for stress reduction, enhanced creativity, and increased long-term productivity.

2. **Reflection and Clarity:**

When you take time for yourself, you can reflect on your experiences, evaluate your decisions, and gain greater clarity about future directions.

3. **Emotional Connection:**

Time spent alone can also be a valuable opportunity to reconnect with your emotions, developing greater emotional awareness.

Practical Strategies for Setting Boundaries:

1. **Proactive Planning:**

Just as you schedule work activities, book "non-negotiable" moments for yourself in your calendar. It could be an hour of reading, an afternoon of walks, or a weekend getaway.

2. **Clear Communication:**

When discussing your boundaries with others, be clear and direct. This helps prevent misunderstandings and sets realistic expectations.

3. **Mental Exercises:**

If you feel guilty or anxious about setting boundaries, consider practicing meditations or visualizations that strengthen your sense of autonomy and security.

4. **Community Support:**

Surround yourself with people who understand and respect your need to set boundaries. This support can come from support groups, friends, family, or therapists.

Energy Management and Boundary Setting:

Effective time management is often praised, but what's equally crucial is energy management. Even if you have the time to do something, without the necessary energy, your efficiency and productivity will suffer.

1. **Recognize Energy Cycles:**

Pay attention to the times of day when you feel most energetic and when you tend to feel more tired. This awareness allows you to schedule activities strategically.

2. **Prioritization and Focus:**

Consider your priorities and focus your energy on what truly matters. Learning to recognize and, if necessary, decline secondary or non-essential activities.

The Value of Authenticity in Setting Boundaries:

Many people avoid setting boundaries for fear of appearing selfish or disappointing others. However, being authentic about your needs and capabilities can strengthen relationships and lead to greater reciprocity.

1. Authenticity and Expectations:

Being clear about your limits helps set realistic expectations, avoiding frustrations and misunderstandings.

2. Setting Boundaries as an Act of Transparency:

Communicating your boundaries shows that you're someone who values honesty and clarity, characteristics often appreciated both personally and professionally.

The Impact of Boundaries on Mental Health:

Constant exposure to stress and pressure can lead to exhaustion, burnout, and other mental health challenges. Setting boundaries is not only a way to protect your time but also to protect your mind.

1. Preventing Burnout:

Inability to set boundaries can lead to burnout, with symptoms ranging from constant fatigue to a loss of interest in daily activities.

2. Self-Esteem and Boundaries:

Every time you assert your boundaries, you reinforce the message that your needs and well-being are important. This can improve self-esteem and self-worth.

Practical Methods for Setting and Maintaining Boundaries:

1. Active Listening Techniques:

When someone makes a request, take a moment to truly understand what's being asked before responding. This gives you time to evaluate if you can or want to comply with the request.

2. Strategic Deferral:

If you're unsure about your ability or willingness to fulfill a request, consider asking for some time to think about it. For example, "Can I get back to you tomorrow?"

3. Hone Your Intuition:

Develop the ability to tune in to yourself and recognize when something crosses your boundaries, even if it may seem like a reasonable request on the surface.

Conclusion:

Boundaries are essential for maintaining balance in life and ensuring that your needs and priorities are respected. Through self-reflection, awareness, and effective communication, you can learn to set boundaries that protect your energy, time, and mental health, leading to a more harmonious and fulfilling life.

11. Physical Exercise and Movement

Benefits of Sports and Physical Activity:

Physical exercise is not only beneficial for the body but also offers a range of advantages for the mind. Here are some key reasons why sports and physical activity are essential:

1. Release of Endorphins:

Physical exercise stimulates the production of endorphins, known as "happiness hormones." These chemicals act as natural painkillers and can improve mood.

2. Stress Reduction:

Physical activity can help reduce cortisol, the stress hormone, in the body, promoting a sense of calm and well-being.

3. Improved Sleep:

Regular exercise can contribute to better sleep quality, helping you feel more rested and rejuvenated.

4. Enhancement of Memory and Cognitive Abilities:

Regular physical exercise can improve brain function and protect against age-related cognitive decline.

5. Boosting Self-Esteem:

Improving fitness and achieving personal goals in physical activity can contribute to a better sense of self-esteem and personal fulfillment.

Specific Mind Exercises:

Not all exercises are purely physical. Some are specifically designed to empower the mind or offer psychological benefits:

1. Yoga:

In addition to improving flexibility and strength, yoga emphasizes awareness of the present moment and the connection between mind and body. Poses and breathing help calm the mind and reduce stress.

2. Tai Chi:

This ancient Chinese martial art, often described as "meditation in motion," helps improve balance, coordination, and body awareness. It is also known for reducing stress and enhancing concentration.

3. Dance:

Dancing not only provides a cardiovascular workout but also offers the opportunity to express yourself and release emotions. Music and rhythm can have a soothing effect on the mind.

4. Nature Walks:

Walking outdoors, especially in natural environments like forests or parks, can have beneficial effects on mental well-being. Connecting with nature helps reduce stress and improve mood.

5. Stretching and Pilates:

These practices improve flexibility and posture while also helping relax the mind. Focusing on breath and mindful movement promotes inner peace.

Neurological Effects of Exercise:

The brain greatly benefits from physical activity. Exercise not only produces cellular changes but also stimulates the release of neurotransmitters and hormones that can have a profound impact on our mental state.

1. Neuroplasticity:

Physical exercise promotes neuroplasticity, the brain's ability to rewire and create new neural connections. This can aid cognitive ability and memory.

2. Neurogenesis:

Studies have shown that exercise, particularly cardiovascular training, can stimulate neurogenesis, the creation of new nerve cells, especially in the hippocampus, a key region for memory and learning.

The Mind-Body Connection:

1. Body-Mind Feedback:

When your body feels good and active, it sends positive signals to the brain. Similarly, a healthy mind promotes a healthy body. This feedback loop can be enhanced through regular exercise.

2. Grounding:

Some exercises, like walking barefoot on grass or sand, can provide a grounding experience, connecting the individual to the present and the Earth. This can have calming and rebalancing effects.

The Role of Exercise in Preventing Mental Illness:

1. Depression Prevention:

In addition to endorphin release, regular exercise can reduce the risk of developing depression due to its effects on neurotransmitter balance and promotion of neurogenesis.

2. Anxiety Management:

Physical activity can reduce anxiety symptoms by providing an outlet for accumulated tensions and improving the regulation of the nervous system.

Exercise as Moving Meditation:

1. Flow and Concentration:

Activities like running, cycling, or swimming can lead to a state of "flow" where individuals are fully immersed in the activity, often losing track of time.

This deep concentration is similar to meditative states.

2. Martial Arts:

In addition to Tai Chi, many other martial arts disciplines, such as Karate, Judo, or Aikido, emphasize the connection between mind, body, and spirit. Regular practice can help develop concentration, discipline, and mindfulness.

The Importance of Consistency:

1. Daily Routine:

Even small movements, when done regularly, can make a difference. You don't need intense workouts every day; even a short walk or some stretching exercises can be beneficial.

2. Finding Enjoyable Activities:

The key to maintaining a long-term exercise routine is finding activities you love, whether it's dancing, walking in the park, swimming, or anything else that makes you feel good.

Conclusion:

While many embark on fitness journeys to improve their outward appearance, the inner benefits, especially for the mind and psychological well-being, are immense and sometimes overlooked. Integrating exercise as a fundamental part of self-care can have profound and lasting effects on quality of life.

12. Writing to Free the Mind

Journaling and Reflection:

1. The Power of Journaling:

Writing in a journal can be a powerful tool for self-reflection. It allows you to express thoughts and feelings, giving them a concrete form and, at times, helping make sense of what you're experiencing.

2. Daily Rituals:

Establishing a daily writing ritual can be an effective way to free the mind from accumulated worries or tensions throughout the day.

3. Analyzing and Understanding:

Beyond being an outlet, journaling can serve as a tool for analyzing situations, behaviors, or feelings. Over time, it can also help recognize patterns or trends in your behavior or way of thinking.

4. Memory and Growth:

Keeping a diary can be a way to document your life, progress, and challenges. Reading past entries can offer valuable insights into your personal growth and evolution.

Therapeutic Writing Techniques:

1. Free Writing:

This technique involves writing freely for a set period (e.g., 10 or 20 minutes) without worrying about grammar, punctuation, or coherence. The goal is to free the mind and allow thoughts to flow freely.

2. Unsent Letters:

Writing a letter to someone (living or deceased) with whom you have unresolved issues or unexpressed feelings can be therapeutic. The key is that this letter will never be sent, giving the freedom to express what you truly feel.

3. Gratitude List:

Focusing on what you're grateful for can change a person's perspective and improve their mood. Writing a regular list of things, people, or experiences you're grateful for can have a positive effect on mood and life perception.

4. Personal Narrative:

Writing a story or narrative based on your life, or creating a narrative that incorporates your feelings and thoughts, can be an effective way to explore and better understand yourself.

5. Writing Prompts:

Sometimes, getting started can be the hardest part. Using writing prompts or guiding questions can help kickstart the reflection and writing process.

The Art of Journaling:

1. Deep Introspection:

Keeping a journal can serve as a mirror to the soul, reflecting feelings, aspirations, and fears. This kind of introspection can help better understand oneself and address unresolved internal issues.

2. Setting Goals:

Writing down your goals, both short-term and long-term, can provide clarity and motivation. Reviewing these goals over time can help monitor progress and adapt to changes.

3. A Journey Through Time:

In addition to documenting the present, a journal can become a valuable archive of your past thoughts and feelings, offering a unique perspective on changes and constants in your life.

Writing as a Refuge:

1. A Safe Space:

A journal can become a private refuge, a place where you can express yourself without judgment, without fear of being misunderstood or criticized.

2. Catharsis Through Words:

Sometimes, the simple act of putting words on paper can lead to a sense of release, allowing you to release accumulated tensions or repressed feelings.

Innovative Methods of Therapeutic Writing:

1. Poetry and Haiku:

Creating poetry or haiku can be an alternative and artistic way to express feelings and thoughts. These brief and conceptual forms can capture the essence of a moment or a feeling in a few words.

2. Self-Dialogue:

Writing a dialogue between the "current self" and the "future self" or the "past self" can offer interesting perspectives and help in decision-making or resolving internal conflicts.

3. Visual Journaling:

Integrating writing with visual elements such as drawings, collages, or photographs can enrich the journaling experience, making it more stimulating and engaging.

4. Mind Maps:

This type of writing, using diagrams and charts, can help visualize ideas, concepts, or feelings, connecting various elements together.

Long-Term Benefits of Writing:

1. Emotional Resilience:

The habit of writing regularly can increase emotional resilience, helping to face future challenges with greater balance and insight.

2. Increased Self-Awareness:

Reviewing old entries can reveal recurring patterns of behavior or reactions, allowing for greater awareness and personal growth.

3. Connection with Others:

Sharing parts of your diary or writings with trusted individuals can create a deeper level of connection and understanding.

Conclusion:

The act of writing is a journey, not only through words but also through the soul. Through various styles and techniques, writing provides access to our inner world, allowing us to explore, understand, and ultimately free the mind. In a world often overwhelmed by external stimuli, writing can become a compass, guiding us toward greater clarity and inner peace.

13. Talking to Someone

Finding a Confidant:

1. The Importance of Sharing:

Sharing thoughts and feelings can provide relief, offering an outlet and an external perspective. The simple act of verbalizing what concerns us can reduce the intensity of emotions.

2. Who Is a Confidant:

A confidant can be a friend, a family member, or anyone you trust. The key element is the confidant's ability to listen without judgment and offer support.

3. Building Trust:

A strong relationship with a confidant is based on trust and mutual understanding. It's essential that both parties feel safe and respected.

4. Benefits of Having a Confidant:

Having someone to share with can lead to greater mental clarity, reduced stress, and improved mood.

Moreover, it can provide a new perspective or solutions to seemingly insurmountable problems.

Benefits of Therapy:

1. A Professional and Neutral Environment:

Therapy provides a safe and neutral environment to freely express feelings and concerns, knowing that what is shared will remain confidential.

2. Tools and Techniques:

Unlike a confidant, a therapist is trained to offer specific tools and techniques to address specific issues, from stress management to trauma resolution.

3. An Objective Perspective:

Therapists offer an external and objective perspective, helping patients see things from a different viewpoint and identify unhealthy patterns or behaviors.

4. Long-Term Support:

While a confidant may offer occasional support, therapy can provide long-term support, helping navigate ongoing challenges or deeply rooted issues.

5. Personalized Approach:

Every individual is unique, and what works for one may not work for another. A therapist can tailor the therapeutic approach to the specific needs of the patient.

The Power of Interpersonal Dialogue:

1. Mirroring Reflection:

When we talk to someone, we often receive back what we have expressed, like in a mirror. This "mirror effect" can help recognize and address feelings or thoughts that might otherwise not be clear.

2. Emotional Validation:

Feeling understood and validated can have therapeutic effects. Recognizing that one's emotions are valid can help reduce feelings of isolation and loneliness.

3. The Benefits of Active Listening:

Having someone who actively listens – that is, who is fully present and attentive – can help clarify confused thoughts and make you feel that what you're saying has value.

Support Groups and Communities:

1. Solidarity and Understanding:

Joining support groups or communities can provide a sense of belonging. Knowing that others are facing similar challenges can offer comfort and perspective.

2. Learning Through Others:

Listening to others' experiences can provide new ideas or approaches to personal problems. Others' stories can inspire and offer hope.

3. Giving and Receiving:

In such groups, you not only receive support but also have the opportunity to provide support to others, creating a cycle of empathy and understanding.

Considerations on Group Therapy:

1. Group Dynamics:

Group therapy offers an environment where individuals with similar challenges can share and learn together. Group interactions can provide valuable insights into one's situation.

2. Multiple Feedback:

Unlike individual therapy, where feedback comes solely from the therapist, group therapy offers the opportunity to receive feedback from multiple perspectives.

3. Cost-Effective:

Group therapy can often be more economically accessible than individual therapy.

Technologies and Talking:

1. Online Therapy:

With the advent of digital technologies, it's now possible to access therapy remotely, allowing anyone with an internet connection to find support.

2. Mental Wellness Apps:

Numerous applications have been developed to offer mindfulness tools, emotional diaries, and even therapeutic chatbots.

Conclusion:

Communication, at its core, is one of the most powerful tools for emotional processing. It provides a way to navigate the intricacies of the mind and find clarity amid chaos. Through various modes – both personal and group, offline and online – the ability to speak and be heard is a fundamental component on the journey to self-understanding and mental well-being. In an increasingly interconnected world, opportunities to connect and find support are abundant, offering hope and solutions to anyone facing the challenges of overthinking.

14. Time Management and Organization

Planning Techniques:

1. The "Three Ps" Method:

- **Plan:** Start the day with a clear list of tasks to complete. Avoid overloading the list; keep it realistic.

- **Prioritize:** Identify the most important or urgent tasks and tackle them first.

- **Pace (Rhythm):** Spread tasks throughout the day to avoid feeling overwhelmed.

2. Pomodoro Technique:

- This technique involves working intensely for 25 minutes and then taking a 5-minute break. This helps maintain high concentration and reduces fatigue.

3. Calendars and Planners:

- Use physical or digital calendars and planners to track appointments and deadlines.

4. Long-Term Planning:

- In addition to daily planning, consider weekly, monthly, or yearly planning to gain an overview of commitments and goals.

Avoiding Procrastination:

1. Understanding the Causes:

- Identify what is causing procrastination. It could be fear, perfectionism, lack of motivation, or other personal reasons.

2. The "Five-Minute" Technique:

- Instead of thinking about completing an entire task, commit to working on it for just five minutes. Once you start, you may find the desire to continue beyond that short period.

3. Task Breakdown:

- Divide larger tasks into smaller, manageable sub-tasks. This makes starting much less daunting.

4. Create a Supportive Environment:

- Ensure your workspace is free from distractions. This may involve cleaning your desk, disabling notifications, or choosing a quiet place to work.

5. Reward Yourself:

- Establish small rewards for yourself once a task is completed or a milestone is reached. This can serve as additional motivation.

Advanced Planning Techniques:

1. Mind Maps:

- These visual diagrams can help visualize tasks, ideas, and goals, making organization and planning easier. By drawing branches extending from a central idea, you can get an overview of activities and subtasks.

2. Batch Method:

- Group similar tasks and complete them together. For example, if you have several emails to send, you might decide to do them all in one time block.

3. Weekly Review:

- Dedicate time at the end of each week to reflect on what you've accomplished, what you haven't, and plan for the following week. This can prevent the feeling of being overwhelmed by accumulated tasks.

In-Depth Procrastination Strategies:

1. Self-Compromise:

- If a task seems too large or daunting, negotiate a compromise with yourself. For example, if you can't commit to an hour of intense study, commit to 20 minutes.

2. Visualization:

- Imagine the feeling of having completed the task. This perspective can provide a motivational boost to get started.

3. "Eat the Frog" Method:

- This method is based on the idea that starting the day by completing the most challenging task (the "frog") makes everything else seem easier by comparison.

4. Cost-Benefit Analysis:

- When tempted to procrastinate, list the costs of that choice and the benefits of taking action. This can help you see things in perspective and prioritize tasks.

Using Technology to Your Advantage:

1. Time Management Apps:

- There are numerous applications designed to assist with planning, such as Trello, Asana, or Todoist. These apps can help organize tasks, set reminders, and track progress.

2. Timers and Stopwatches:

- Using timers or stopwatches to set time limits for tasks can help maintain focus and prevent time-wasting.

3. Distraction Blockers:

- If you find yourself distracted by websites or applications, consider using software like "Freedom" or "Cold Turkey" to limit access to these temptations during work periods.

Conclusion:

The art of time management and organization is not just about tools or methods but also about mindset. It requires self-awareness, reflection, and sometimes a dose of self-discipline. While techniques can provide structure and direction, the most important element is intention: a genuine desire to live more intentionally and productively, avoiding the traps of overthinking and procrastination. With the right balance of strategies and the willingness to apply them, it is possible not only to manage your time more effectively but also to live with greater presence and purpose.

15. Learning to Embrace Uncertainty

Letting Go of the Need for Control:

1. Recognizing the Illusion of Total Control:

- No one has absolute control over every aspect of their life. Recognizing that many events and circumstances are beyond our control can be liberating.

2. Reflecting on the Past:

- Recall past moments when you worried excessively about something, and in the end, everything turned out fine, or you learned from the experience. This reflection can help you relax in the present.

3. Practicing Resilience:

- Instead of trying to control every situation, develop your ability to adapt and respond effectively to challenges. Resilience allows you to confront uncertainty with an open and flexible mindset.

4. Define What You Can Control:

- Focus on your actions, reactions, and attitudes. These are areas of your life where you have real control. Channeling your energy into these aspects can be much more productive.

Living in the Present:

1. Mindfulness and Meditation:

- Mindfulness practice encourages you to focus on the present moment. Through meditation, you can learn to observe your thoughts without judgment, allowing you to detach from future worries.

2. Immersive Activities:

- Find activities that fully engage your attention, such as art, reading, or gardening. These activities can function as a form of meditation, anchoring you in the present.

3. Grounding Exercises:

- When feeling overwhelmed, try grounding techniques. A common exercise is to identify five things you can see, four you can touch, three you can hear, two you can smell, and one you can taste. This helps center you in the present.

4. Acknowledge the Beauties of the Moment:

- Take a moment each day to recognize and appreciate the small joys and beauties of your daily life. It could be a shared smile, a natural landscape, or a moment of tranquility.

Embracing Vulnerability:

1. Humanity in Vulnerability:

- Recognizing and accepting your vulnerability can be key to building deeper and more authentic relationships. Admitting that we don't have all the answers can bring others closer, as it reveals our authentic humanity.

2. Growth from Vulnerability:

- Often, life's deepest lessons emerge from moments when we feel most vulnerable and uncertain. These periods can catalyze significant personal growth.

3. Strength in Acceptance:

- While society may often associate vulnerability with weakness, accepting your vulnerability can actually be a sign of incredible strength. It demonstrates the ability to confront your fears and progress despite them.

Celebrate Small Victories:

1. Small Steps:

- When faced with uncertainty, focusing on small, achievable steps or goals can make an overwhelming situation more manageable. Each small victory can boost self-confidence.

2. Record of Achievements:

- Keeping a record of achievements, even minor ones, can provide a source of motivation and a reminder of the progress made, especially during times of doubt.

Review Your Expectations:

1. Adaptability:

- Often, distress arises when reality doesn't meet our expectations. Reviewing and adjusting your expectations to align with reality can help reduce tension and frustration.

2. Realistic Expectations:

- Set expectations that take into account reality and unforeseeable factors. This doesn't mean lowering standards but rather being realistic and flexible in how you approach goals.

Establish an Anchor of Serenity:

1. Find Your 'Constant':

- Even amidst chaos, having a "constant" in your life—whether it's a routine, a loved one, or a personal practice—can provide comfort and stability.

2. Moments of Silence:

- Dedicate time every day, even just a few minutes, to be in silence and center yourself. This can serve as a rejuvenating pause and an opportunity to reconnect with yourself.

Conclusion:

Living in an unpredictable world requires a new set of skills and mindset. It's not about preparing for every eventuality but rather developing the ability to navigate gracefully through life's uncertain waters. Through acceptance, vulnerability, and embracing uncertainty, we can find not only peace but also a depth of experience and connection that may not have been possible otherwise.

16. Art and Creativity as Outlet

Expression as Liberation:

1. Art as a Reflection of the Soul:

- Art and creativity represent not only a means to express thoughts and emotions but also to explore the very essence of our being. Through art, we can delve into the depths of our psyche, confront fears or traumas, and find solutions to inner dilemmas.

2. Channeling Emotions:

- When overwhelmed by overthinking, art can serve as a channel to release such energies, transforming frantic thoughts into tangible works.

Psychological and Physical Benefits:

1. Stress Reduction:

- Artistic creation can induce a meditative-like state, reducing cortisol levels (the stress hormone) and promoting relaxation.

2. Boosting Self-Esteem:

- Completing a work of art provides a sense of accomplishment, strengthening self-confidence and one's own abilities.

3. Brain Stimulation:

- Art and creativity stimulate the brain in unique ways, promoting neuroplasticity and enhancing functions such as memory, concentration, and problem-solving skills.

Finding Your Artistic Voice:

1. Explore Different Art Forms:

- Whether it's painting, sculpture, writing, dance, music, or photography, it's essential to explore different art forms to discover which resonates most with your inner self.

2. Create Without Judgment:

- Art should not be an activity constrained by external expectations or judgments. It's a pure form of personal expression, and every individual should feel free to create without the fear of being judged.

3. Courses and Workshops:

- Enrolling in local courses or workshops can be an excellent way to learn new techniques, find inspiration, and connect with other art enthusiasts.

Art Therapy:

1. Art Psychology:

- Some therapists use art as a means to help patients explore and express emotions that may be difficult to verbalize. This form of therapy can provide a unique perspective on an individual's issues and help them find ways to address them.

2. Colors and Emotions:

- Colors can profoundly influence our emotions. The practice of intentionally choosing specific colors during artistic creation can serve both as self-exploration and as a means to influence one's mood.

Sensory Connections in Art:

1. Tactility in Sculpture:

- Shaping clay or sculpting can be incredibly therapeutic. Physical connection with the material allows for a form of expression that can be profoundly liberating.

2. Music and Rhythm:

- Creating or listening to music can influence our mental well-being. Rhythm, in particular, can have a direct impact on our mood, offering a form of moving meditation.

Creative Rituals and Routine:

1. The Importance of Routine:

- Establishing a creative routine can help provide a sense of structure and purpose. This ritual can become a sacred moment in the day, an opportunity to disconnect and connect with oneself.

2. Personal Creative Spaces:

- Having a dedicated corner or room for art and creativity can foster inspiration. This space can become a sanctuary, a place to retreat to and feel free to express oneself.

Art in Everyday Life:

1. Integrating Art:

- You don't need to be an "artist" to integrate art into everyday life. Even simple activities like doodling during a call or creatively cooking can be ways to express yourself.

2. Digital Arts and New Media:

- With the rise of technology, opportunities for artistic creation have expanded. Graphics, digital photography, and virtual reality offer new platforms to explore and share creativity.

Conclusion:

Art is much more than a pastime or a profession; it is a universal language, a vehicle for exploring the human being, and a means to connect with one's deepest self. Through regular practice and immersion in creativity, we can not only find relief from the pressures of daily life but also discover new horizons of self-understanding and personal growth. In a world where overthinking is increasingly common, art emerges as a beacon of hope, offering a path to serenity and inner balance.

17. Limiting Stimulant Intake

The Chemistry of Stimulants and the Nervous System:

1. Coffee and Caffeine:

- Caffeine is a powerful central nervous system stimulant. It temporarily increases energy and alertness. However, excessive intake can lead to nervousness, insomnia, tachycardia, and, in some individuals, anxiety or panic attacks.

2. Alcohol:

- While many people use alcohol as a way to relax, it can actually have the opposite effect. If consumed in excess, alcohol can alter serotonin levels and other neurotransmitters in the brain, exacerbating anxiety and reducing the body's ability to handle stress.

3. Sugars:

Refined sugars, such as those found in sugary beverages, sweets, and many processed foods, can cause rapid spikes and crashes in blood glucose levels. These fluctuations can lead to symptoms like nervousness, irritability, and mental fatigue.

Cumulative Effects of Stimulants:

1. Dependence and Tolerance:

With regular consumption of stimulants like caffeine, the body can develop tolerance, leading people to consume increasing amounts to achieve the same effects. This dependence can worsen anxiety and overthinking symptoms.

2. Interaction of Stimulants:

When multiple stimulants are consumed together, such as coffee and sugar, their effects can add up and amplify. This can lead to a heightened sense of restlessness and nervousness.

Healthy Choices and Alternatives:

1. Teas and Herbs:

Many teas, like green tea, contain lower amounts of caffeine compared to coffee. Additionally, there are herbal teas like chamomile and passionflower tea known for their relaxing properties.

2. Gradual Reduction:

Instead of abruptly eliminating stimulants, consider reducing them gradually. This can help prevent withdrawal symptoms like headaches or irritability.

3. Choose Natural Sweeteners:

Instead of refined sugars, consider more natural alternatives like honey, maple syrup, or stevia sweetener.

17. Limiting Stimulant Intake

Understanding the Biochemistry of Stimulants:

1. Adenosine and Caffeine:

Caffeine primarily works by blocking adenosine receptors in the brain. Adenosine is a neurotransmitter that promotes sleep and relaxation. When blocked by caffeine, one experiences a sense of alertness, but this can also contribute to feelings of anxiety.

2. Alcohol and GABA:

Alcohol acts by increasing the effect of GABA (gamma-aminobutyric acid), an inhibitory neurotransmitter. While in the short term, this can produce a feeling of relaxation, in the long term, it can alter the production and function of GABA, leading to increased anxiety when alcohol wears off.

3. Sugars and Insulin:

Excessive sugar intake can cause rapid spikes in insulin. These spikes and subsequent crashes can affect mood and concentration, predisposing the brain to cycles of overthinking.

Psychological Implications of Stimulants:

1. Alteration of Perception:

Stimulants, especially alcohol, can distort one's perception of reality, making it difficult to distinguish between realistic and irrational thoughts, fueling the cycle of overthinking.

2. Negative Reinforcement:

If a person relies on stimulants to manage stress or anxiety, a cycle of negative reinforcement can develop. The individual may begin to believe they need the stimulant to feel better, even without addressing the underlying cause of their distress.

Alternatives and Substitutions:

1. Flavored Water:

If you find yourself consuming sugary or caffeinated beverages for the taste, try substituting with naturally flavored water with fresh fruit or herbs.

2. Herbal Teas:

There are numerous caffeine-free tea options that can provide flavor without the stimulating effect. Teas like rooibos, chamomile, or mint-based herbal teas can be a good alternative.

3. Whole Foods:

Reduce refined sugars by choosing whole foods. Eating items like fruits, vegetables, whole grains, and lean proteins can help stabilize blood sugar levels and provide sustained energy.

Stimulants can have a profound impact on our mental state. Understanding how they work in the body and their effects on our minds can help us make more informed choices. Limiting or moderating our intake, along with adopting healthier alternatives, can contribute to greater mental clarity and a reduction in overthinking.

18. The Power of Sleep

The Fundamental Importance of Sleep:

Sleep represents a fundamental pillar of physical and mental well-being. During sleep, the body regenerates, cells repair themselves, and the brain processes the day's information, consolidating memories. Inadequate sleep can compromise these essential functions and leave individuals tired, irritable, and, crucially for our topic, prone to overthinking.

How Overthinking Impacts Sleep:

1. Thought Cycles and Insomnia:

When the mind is inundated with incessant thoughts, falling asleep can become extremely difficult. Overthinking can lead to insomnia or sleep interruptions.

2. Disruption of REM Phases:

Excessive thinking can also influence the REM (Rapid Eye Movement) phases of sleep, which are essential for mental health and memory.

3. Stress and Cortisol:

The anxiety and stress resulting from overthinking can lead to increased cortisol production, a stress hormone, which can delay or disrupt the natural sleep cycle.

Creating a Sleep Routine:

1. Tranquil Environment:

Ensure your bedroom is quiet, dark, and cool. Invest in blackout curtains, use earplugs, or a white noise machine if necessary.

2. Establish a Regular Schedule:

Try to go to bed and wake up at the same time every day, even on weekends. This stabilizes your internal biological clock.

3. Pre-Sleep Ritual:

Establish a relaxing pre-sleep ritual, such as reading a book, listening to calm music, taking a warm bath, or practicing breathing exercises.

4. Digital Detox:

Avoid bright screens (smartphones, computers, TVs) at least an hour before bedtime. The blue light emitted by screens can interfere with the production of melatonin, the sleep hormone.

5. Food and Beverages:

Avoid heavy meals, caffeine, and alcohol before bedtime. While alcohol may make you feel sleepy, it can disrupt sleep during the night.

6. Physical Exercise:

Physical activity during the day can help you sleep better at night. However, try to avoid intense exercises in the evening.

Sleep and Cognitive Health:

Sleep is not just a "shut-off switch" for the body but a vital period of maintenance and repair for the mind.

1. Neurological Processes:

During sleep, glial cells in the brain clear neurological debris, a vital process for maintaining neuronal health and preventing neurodegenerative diseases like Alzheimer's.

2. Memory Consolidation:

During sleep, the brain "rehearses" information learned during the day, consolidating memories and moving information from short-term to long-term memory.

3. Creativity and Problem Solving:

Many individuals find solutions to problems or creative ideas after a good night's sleep. This is because the brain reevaluates and connects different pieces of information during the REM stages of sleep.

Long-Term Effects of Sleep Deprivation:

Chronic lack of sleep can lead to a range of short-term and long-term issues.

1. Reduction in Cognitive Abilities:

Lack of sleep can reduce attention, concentration, and decision-making abilities.

2. Mood Problems:

Chronic insomnia can increase the risk of mood disorders such as depression and anxiety.

3. Weakening of the Immune System:

Failure to regenerate during sleep can lead to a weakened immune system, making the body more susceptible to illnesses and infections.

Additional Tips to Improve Sleep Quality:

1. Mattress and Pillows:

Invest in a good mattress and pillows to ensure proper support and sleep position.

2. Room Fragrance:

Using essential oils like lavender can create a more relaxing environment and promote better sleep.

3. Relaxation Therapies:

Techniques like progressive muscle relaxation or listening to nature sounds can help with falling asleep more easily.

4. Reduce Daytime Naps:

If you find yourself taking frequent daytime naps, it might negatively impact nighttime sleep quality. If necessary, limit daytime naps to 20-30 minutes in the early afternoon.

Conclusion:

Actively working to improve both the quality and quantity of sleep can not only reduce overthinking but also lead to overall improved well-being, increased productivity, mental clarity, and enhanced physical and emotional health. Consider sleep an investment in your health and overall well-being.

19. Establishing a Daily Routine

The Benefits of a Routine:

1. Predictability and Structure:

A routine provides a sense of normalcy and predictability in daily life, reducing anxiety and uncertainty.

2. Improved Efficiency:

With a well-established routine, you save time and mental energy by not constantly thinking about what to do next. This reduces procrastination and increases productivity.

3. Reinforcement of Positive Habits:

When we repeat certain activities every day, they become habits. A well-planned routine can help establish healthy habits.

4. Regulation of Circadian Rhythms:

A daily routine, especially a consistent sleep routine, can help regulate the body's circadian rhythms, improving sleep and daytime energy.

5. Sense of Accomplishment:

Completing planned activities in a routine provides a sense of satisfaction and achievement, boosting self-esteem.

Creating a Calming Routine:

1. Start with a Morning Routine:

Dedicate the first moments of the day to yourself. This could include meditation, breathing exercises, physical activity, or simply reading a book.

2. Relaxing Lunch Break:

Avoid working while eating. Use this time for a real break, perhaps taking a short walk or doing quick stretching exercises.

3. "Me-Time" Slot:

Allocate time every day to do something you love or find relaxing, whether it's listening to music, taking a warm bath, or writing in your journal.

4. Digital Detox:

Spend an hour or two before bedtime without electronic devices. This can reduce exposure to blue light and improve sleep quality.

5. Evening Routine:

This could include relaxation techniques like reading, meditation, or simple breathing exercises. Creating an evening routine signals to your body that it's time to wind down and prepare for restful sleep.

6. Planning and Review:

Take a moment, perhaps in the evening or early morning, to plan the next day or reflect on the day just passed. This can help put things in perspective and reduce overthinking.

The Connection Between Routine and Reducing Overthinking:

Overthinking often emerges in the absence of clarity when the mind wanders aimlessly, seeking answers or solutions. Establishing a routine provides a clear and defined path for the day, reducing the need for constant decision-making and minimizing moments of uncertainty.

Depth in Specific Routines:

1. Meal Planning:

Planning meals may seem like a minor detail, but it can reduce decision fatigue by eliminating the constant question of "what should I eat today?" This conserves mental energy and reduces food-related overthinking.

2. Personal Development Time:

Include a dedicated time for personal growth or learning. This could involve reading a book, listening to an educational podcast, or watching a documentary. Nourishing the mind can help channel the energy of overthinking into productive avenues.

3. Beauty and Self-Care Rituals:

Creating a beauty or self-care routine can serve as a meditative moment. Whether it's skincare, a hair routine, or a relaxing bath, these moments can become sacred and an opportunity to connect with yourself.

4. Set Alarms and Reminders:

It's not just about waking up in the morning. Setting alarms to remind you of breaks, stretching moments, or even to drink water can ensure you're taking care of yourself and reduce the anxiety of forgetting something.

5. Connect with Nature:

If possible, incorporate outdoor time into your daily routine. It could be a short walk, gardening, or simply having coffee on the porch. Connecting with nature has been shown to reduce cortisol levels and promote mental well-being.

6. Reflective Break:

This can be a moment when you put everything aside, close your eyes, and simply be present. During this break, check in with yourself, notice how you feel, and what's happening in your mind.

Flexibility in the Routine:

While the idea of a routine suggests a rigid structure, it's important to maintain some flexibility. Life can present unexpected situations, and there may be days when you can't follow your routine to the letter. And that's okay. The primary goal is to have a guide that helps you navigate the day with a sense of intention and purpose, rather than being reactive to various stimuli and situations that arise.

Personalized Adjustments and Flexibility:

1. Make Variations:

A routine doesn't have to be rigid. Introducing small variations can help keep things interesting and engaging.

2. Time for Improvisation:

Not everything needs to be planned down to the last detail. Leave spaces in your routine for improvisation and spontaneity.

3. Seasonal Routines:

Adapt your routine to different seasons. For example, you may want to do outdoor exercise in the summer and indoor activities during the winter.

Incorporating Relaxation Techniques:

1. Morning Stretching:

A small set of morning stretching exercises can activate your body and prepare it for the day.

2. Breathing Techniques:

Incorporate breathing techniques into your routine, such as during breaks, to help manage stress and anxiety.

3. Visualization:

Use visualization techniques to mentally prepare for challenging commitments or events during the day.

Assessment and Iteration:

1. Weekly Review:

Take a moment at the end of each week to assess how your routine is affecting your well-being. Make necessary adjustments for the following week.

2. Performance Indicators:

Establish Key Performance Indicators (KPIs) to measure the effectiveness of your routine. These could include stress levels, sleep quality, or daytime energy levels.

3. Feedback from Trusted Individuals:

Share your routine with trusted family or friends and request their feedback. Sometimes an external perspective can offer valuable insights.

Special Cases:

1. For Parents:

If you are a parent, include specific moments in your routine for spending time with your children, relaxing with them, or engaging in educational activities.

2. For Students:

If you are a student, integrate study time into your schedule, but also allocate time for relaxation and social activities. A balanced life helps reduce overthinking.

3. For Professionals:

If you are in the working world, remember to balance office time with activities that help you disconnect and relax.

Conclusion:

Remember, your daily routine is unique to you. It's a flexible framework that should serve and support you, not a rigid set of rules you must adhere to at all costs. It should evolve with you and your needs, supporting a balance between productivity, well-being, and relaxation.

20. Conclusion: The Path to Calm

Reflecting on the Journey:

We've traversed a path of deep introspection and discovery. Overthinking is not just a mental obstacle; it can permeate every aspect of our lives, hindering our well-being, relationships, and productivity. However, as we've explored in each chapter, there are tools and techniques at our disposal to address and overcome this tendency.

Key Points:

Understanding Overthinking: We've delved into the causes, manifestations, and repercussions of excessive rumination. Recognizing the problem is the first step in addressing it.

Strategies and Techniques: From meditation to gratitude, from art to time management, we've explored a wide range of tools that can help you center your mind, calm it, and keep it focused on the present.

Personalization: Every individual is unique, and what works for one person may not work for another.

We've emphasized the importance of adapting these techniques to your own life and needs.

An Invitation to Action:

Now that you're armed with knowledge and tools, we encourage you to take the first step, no matter how small. It could be taking five minutes a day to meditate or writing down three things you're grateful for every evening. The journey to conquering overthinking and embracing calm is a process, not a destination.

Looking Ahead:

The path to calm is one of constant learning and adaptation. There will be good days and not-so-good days. But with every step you take, with every tool you apply, you're getting closer to a more centered, present, and serene life.

A Final Thought:

As in any journey, there will be obstacles and detours. However, determination, commitment, and the willingness to invest in yourself will ensure your success. You have the power to shape your mental reality and live a life free from overthinking. Start today, one small step at a time, and see how far you can go.

And with this, we wish you peace, serenity, and a clear mind on your path to calm. Begin now and embrace every moment.

Summary and Useful Resources

In our journey through understanding and managing overthinking, we've touched on various key aspects and techniques that can help find calm and clarity in everyday life:

Introduction: We explored the nature of overthinking and its effects on mental and physical health.

Causes of Overthinking: We examined how past events, fear of the future, and perfectionism can fuel cycles of excessive rumination.

Connection Between Stress and Overthinking: We analyzed how stress can exacerbate overthinking and the body's response.

The Negative Cycle of Overthinking: We discovered how overthinking can become a self-perpetuating cycle.

Recognizing Overthinking: We learned to identify and monitor signs and symptoms.

Meditation and Mindfulness: We were introduced to the practice of mindfulness and meditation techniques.

Mindful Breathing: We discussed the importance of breath in managing overthinking.

The Practice of Gratitude: We highlighted how focusing on the positive can combat overthinking.

Limiting Distractions: Tips on creating environments conducive to concentration.

Setting Boundaries: The importance of establishing personal boundaries.

Physical Exercise: We discussed the benefits of sports and physical activity for the mind.

Writing to Free the Mind: We were introduced to journaling and therapeutic writing.

Talking to Someone: The value of therapy and confiding in others.

Time Management: Tips on planning and avoiding procrastination.

Embracing Uncertainty: Learning to live in the present and let go of the need for control.

Art and Creativity: We discussed the use of art as a form of expression and coping.

Limiting Stimulants: We analyzed the effect of coffee, alcohol, and sugars on anxiety.

The Power of Sleep: The importance of sleep for mental health.

Daily Routine: We discussed how a routine can promote calm.

Conclusion: Final reflections on the path to calm.

Useful Resources:

- **Mindful.org** - A comprehensive mindfulness website with articles, practices, and courses.

- **Headspace** - A meditation app offering guides and guided sessions for various levels.

- **The National Sleep Foundation** - Provides detailed sleep information and tips for better sleep hygiene.

- **Psychology Today** - A website where you can find local therapists and read articles on various psychology-related topics.

- **The Minimalists** - Tips on reducing distractions and living a simpler life.

We invite you to explore these resources and continue your journey to improve your life. Remember, every step, no matter how small, brings you closer to a calmer and more centered mind. Good luck on your path to serenity and inner peace.

Personal Notes: